Funded by supporters of

Sheffield Hospitals Charity

sheffieldhospitalscharity.org.uk

CW01369662

Dedicated to
Alissa Claire Norton
Forever loved

This book belongs to

....

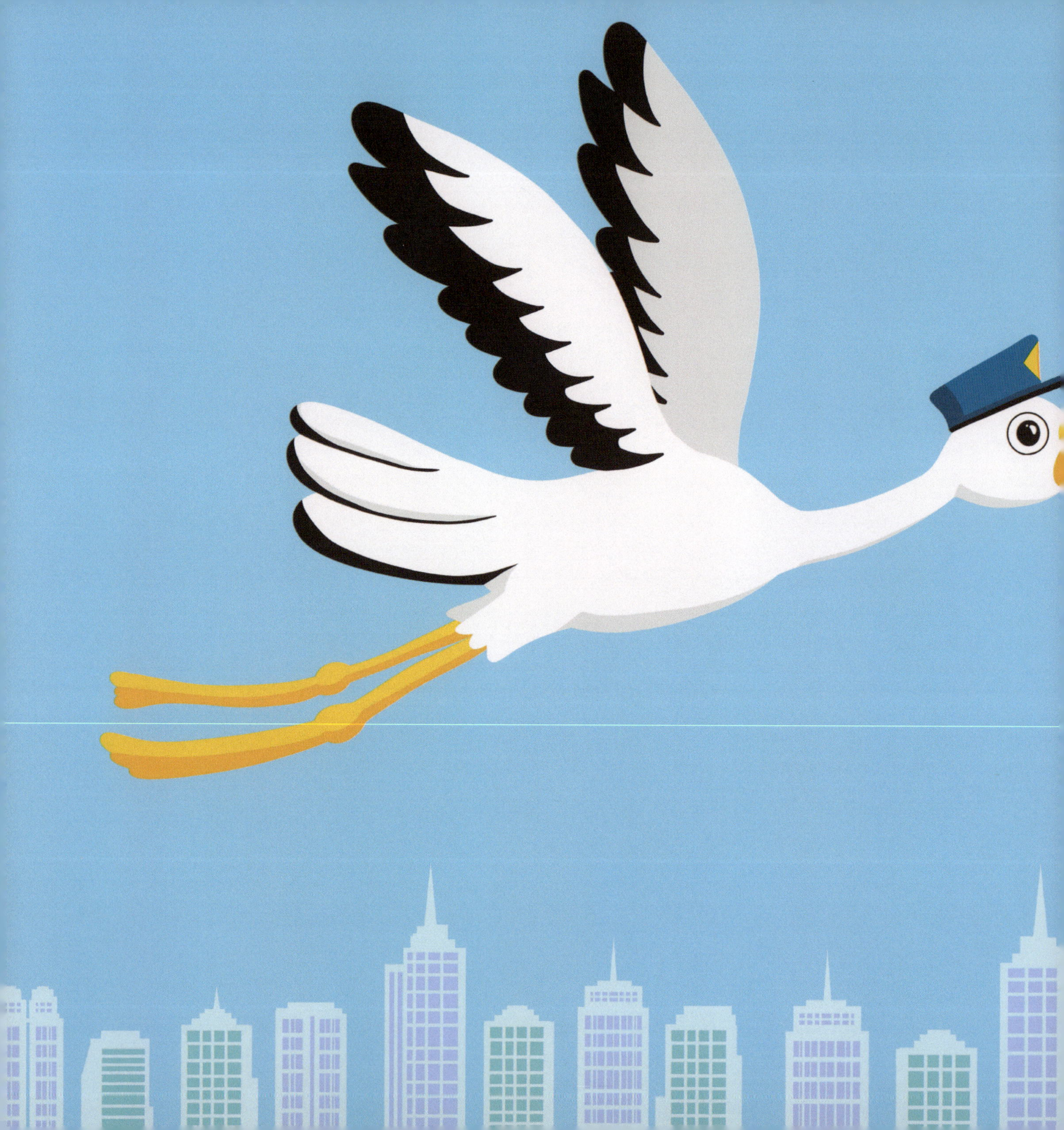

Babies come into the world
In many different ways
Some may come in seconds
And others might take days

Some might come out hairy
And some might come out small

And in some special cases
They don't come to us at all

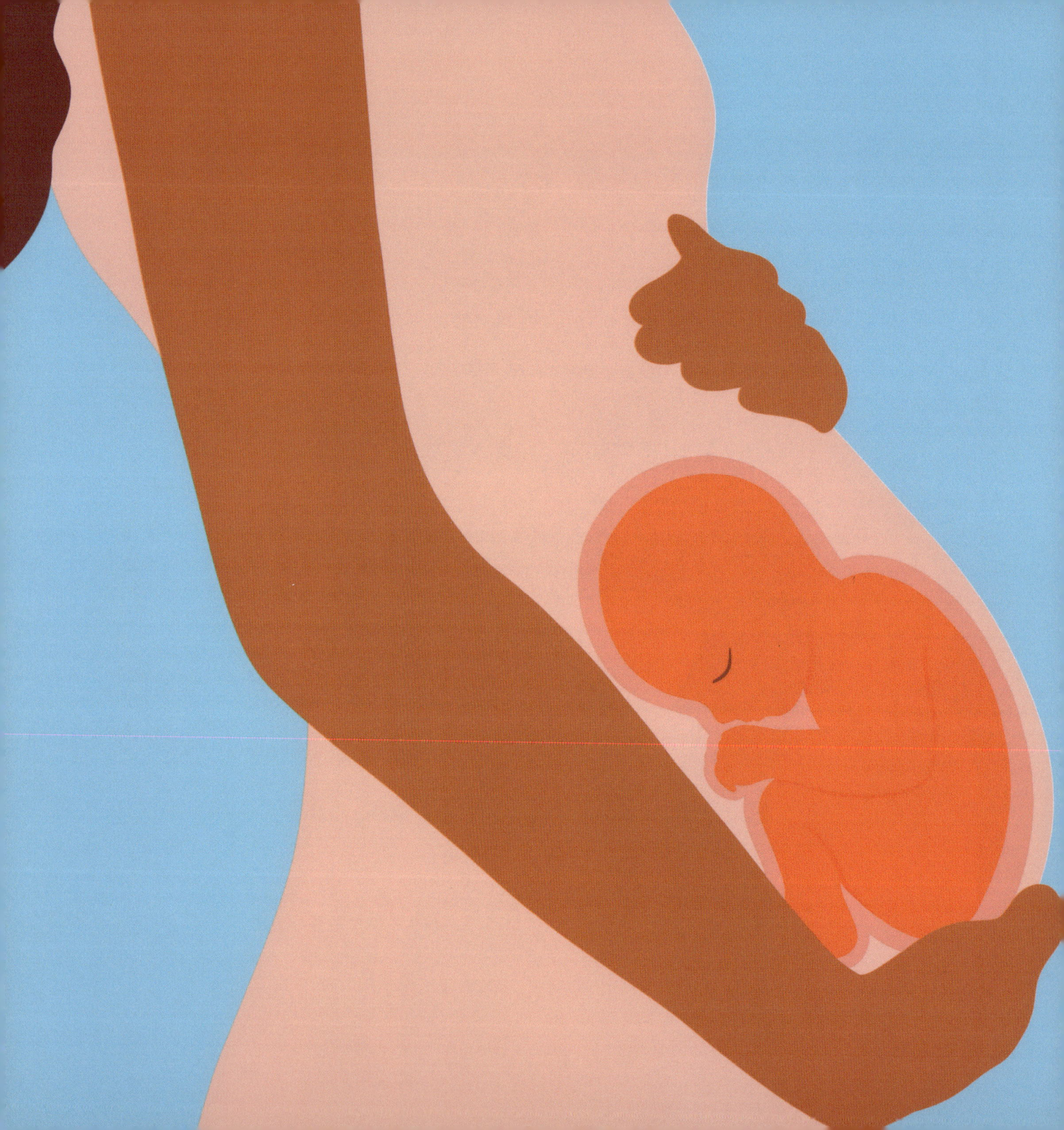

Deep inside the tummy
Where the little baby grows
They grow ten tiny fingers
And a little button nose

But sometimes they stop growing
For a reason we don't know

And with those little babies
we don't get to say "hello"

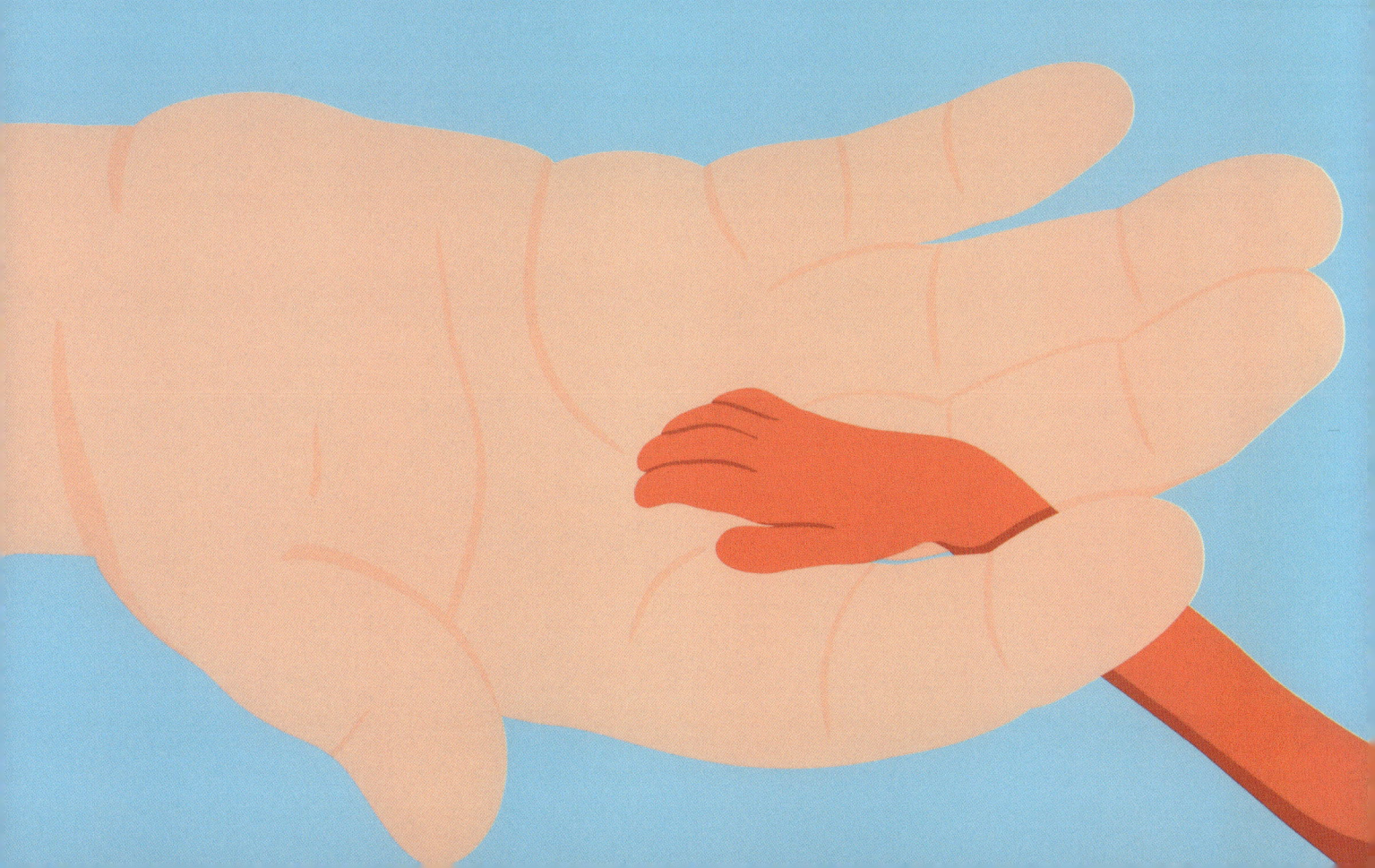

They still have tiny fingers
And tiny baby feet

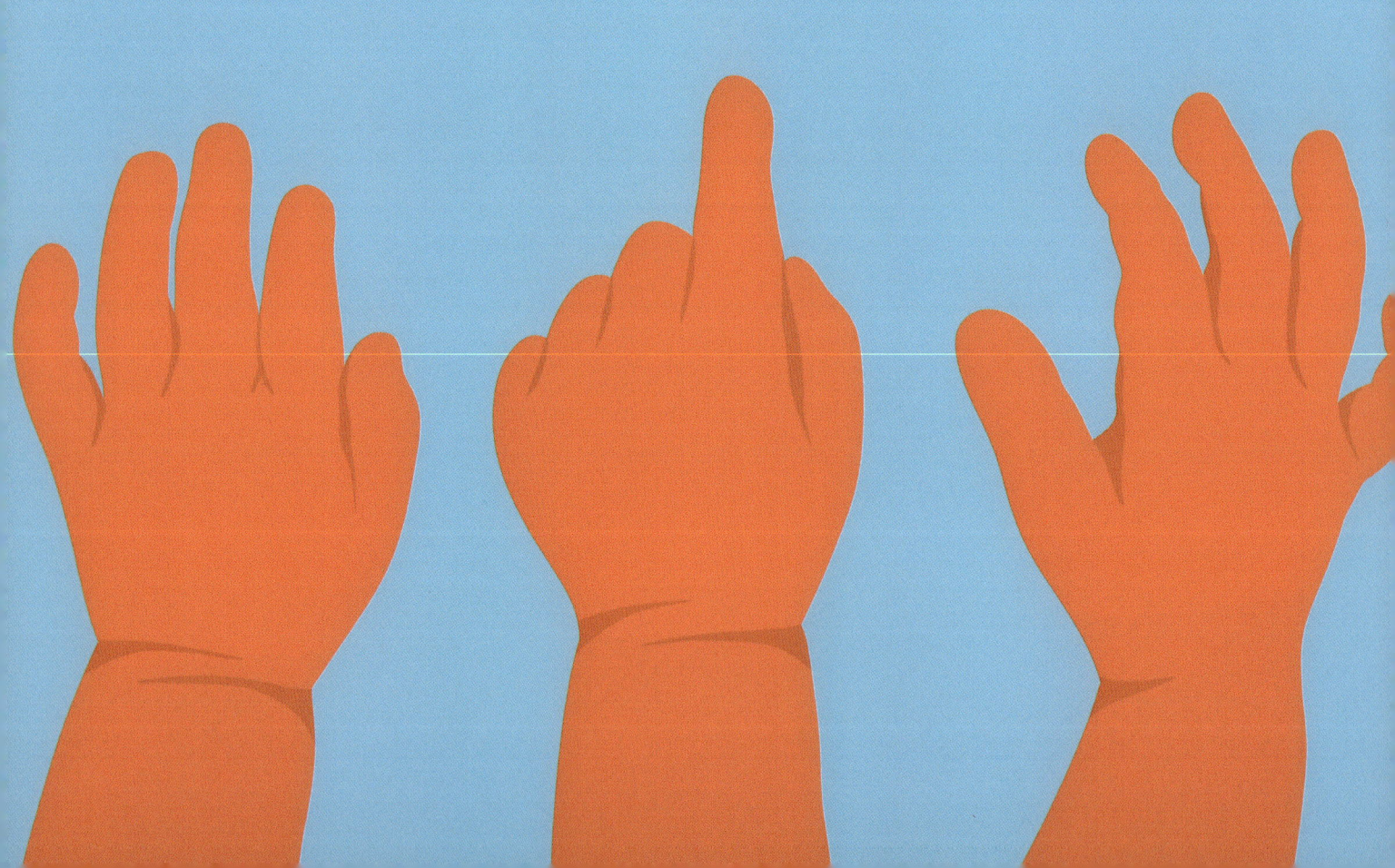

But for some tiny babies
Their hearts no longer beat

So though you cannot hold their hand
Or take them out to play
Know that you are very loved
And everyone's okay

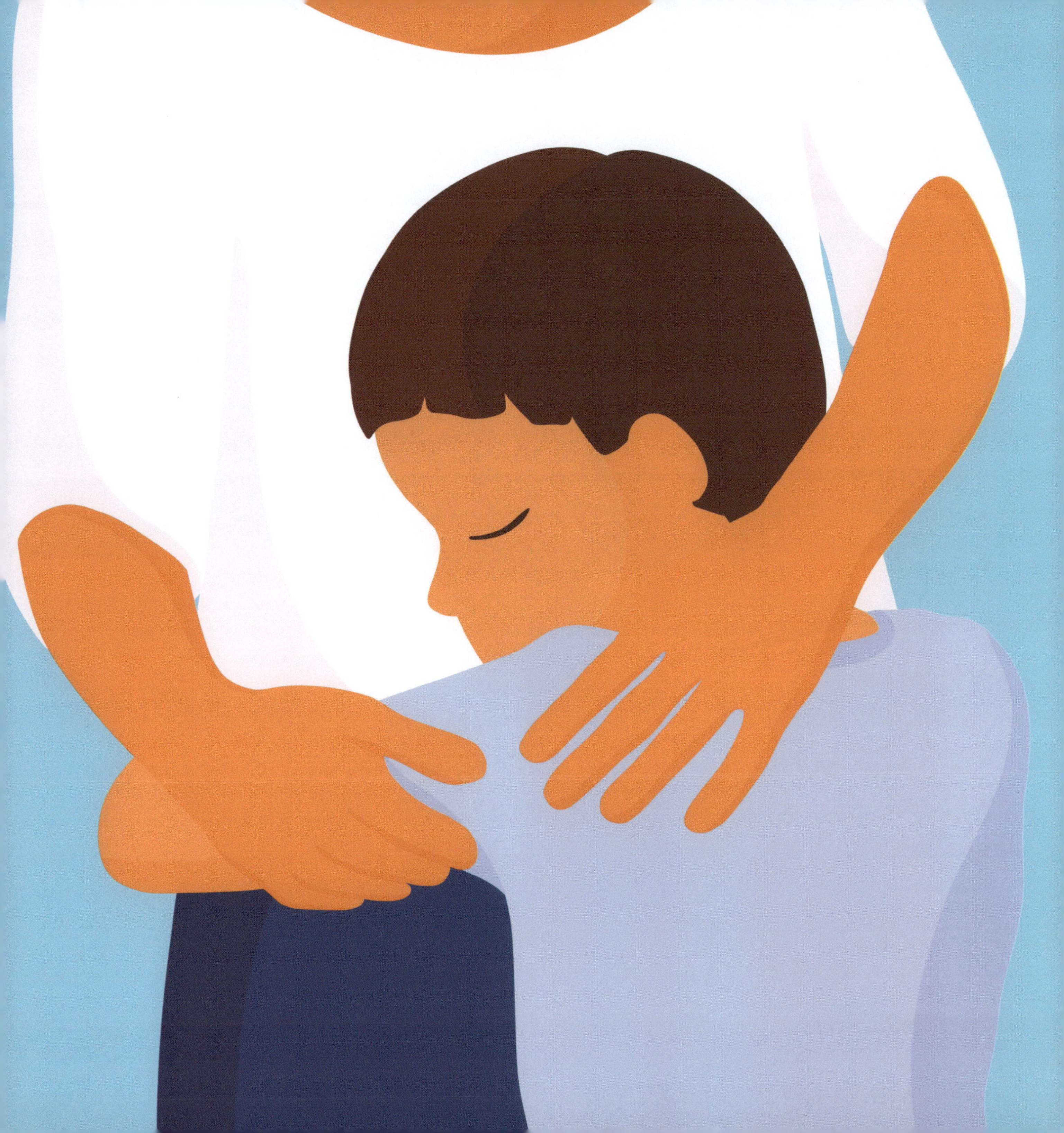

People might seem sad now
You might see people cry

It's normal to get upset when a little baby dies

But we can keep on loving them
Just love them from afar

We'll love them in the house, and bed,
And park, and beach, and car

So when you think of little babies
Remember them with love

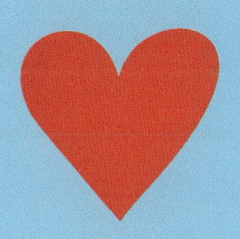

And in return, those babies
They love us from above.

How can you remember little babies?

You could plant a flower for them, light a candle on their birthday, or paint a stone with their name and keep it in a special place.

Printed in Great Britain
by Amazon